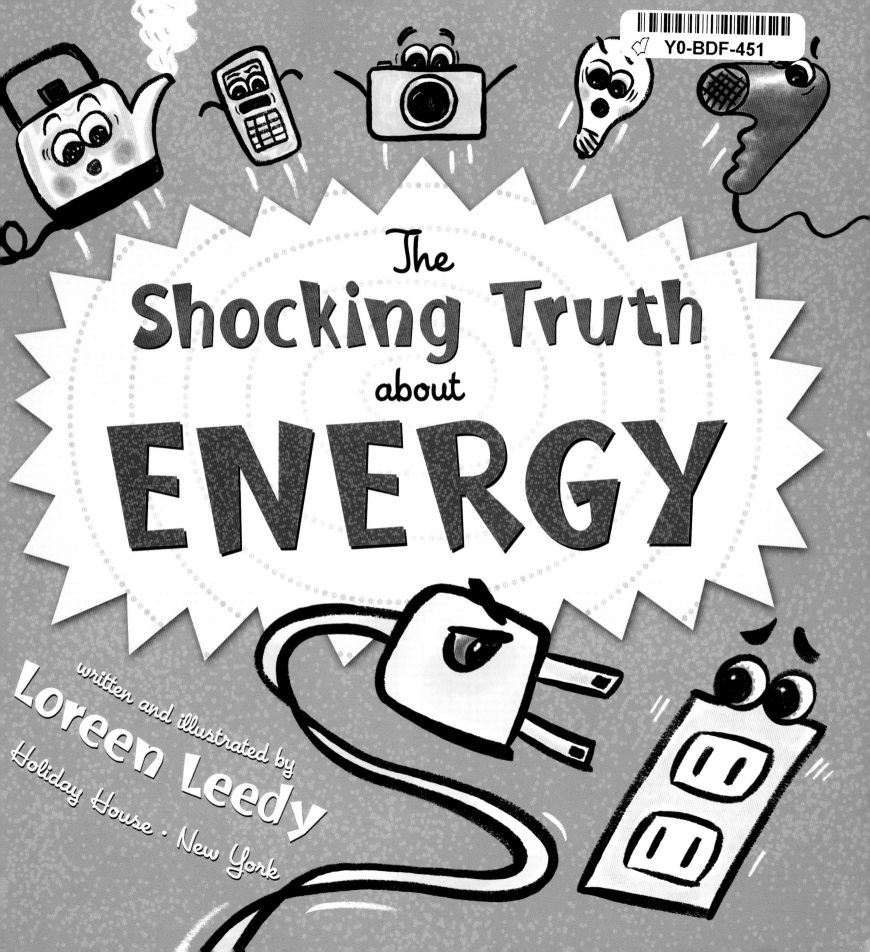

The Shocking Truth about ENERGY

written and illustrated by
Loreen Leedy

Holiday House · New York

The author wishes to thank Dr. D. Mark Riffe
of the Department of Physics at Utah State
University and Dr. Andrew Schuerger of
the Department of Plant Pathology at the
University of Florida for commenting
on the text and sketches prior
to publication.

To a greener future

I'm a big fan
of Erg's!

Library of Congress Cataloging-in-Publication Data
Leedy, Loreen.
The shocking truth about energy / by Loreen Leedy. — 1st ed.
p. cm.
ISBN 978-0-8234-2220-3 (hardcover)
ISBN 978-0-8234-2388-0 (paperback)
1. Power resources—Juvenile literature. 2. Power resources—Environmental aspects—
Juvenile literature. 3. Pollution prevention—Juvenile literature. I. Title.
TJ163.23.L394 2010
333.79—dc22
2009025568

The photo of Earth on page 12 is courtesy of
the National Aeronautics and Space Administration
and the Jet Propulsion Laboratory at Cal Tech.

Hi there!
My name is Erg,
and I'm pure

ENERGY!

Everybody loves
a powerhouse like me.

In fact, people want
more and **more**
ENERGY every day.

That's because I make
everything happen.

I can't do a thing
without Erg!

The funny thing is,
I'm **everywhere**!

The **hard** part is…

SOUND or FUEL or MOTION or ELECTRICITY!

FUEL is stored ENERGY that can be burned. Gasoline, coal, and wood are fuels.

You can't create or destroy ENERGY, but you can change it to another form. Hey, who gets to eat that hot dog?

Burning FUEL (wood) makes HEAT to cook a hot dog.

FUEL

HEAT

Are you wondering how to catch **ME?**

When ENERGY takes the form of a FUEL called **FOOD,** people and animals can **eat** energy.

Inside their bodies, food becomes:

MUSCLE POWER!

I don't have any muscles at all.

If people watch YOU too much, they won't either!

6

Muscles make MOTION.

Muscles can walk, run, fly, jump, dance, hop, sing, crawl, hammer nails, and do a few zillion other things.

But muscles can **fizzle out** pretty fast.

Whew!

BAD NEWS
Muscles **can't** power cars, airplanes, houses, or cities.

GOOD NEWS
Muscle power doesn't pollute.
It's renewable; just eat more food!

This is way too slow.

How long would it take to **push** a car 25 miles using **only** muscle power?

Three days? A week?

A gallon of gasoline can move a car 25 miles in less than an hour!

1 gallon gasoline

That's the power of

FOSSIL FUELS,

such as oil, natural gas, and coal.
They are jam-packed full of ENERGY.

oil (petroleum)

natural gas

coal

Most vehicles run on fuels made from

oil.

Don't be shocked...but fossil fuels are burned to make

ELECTRICITY!

Here's how power plants generate ELECTRICITY:

1. Fuel is burned to heat water.

2. Hot water becomes steam.

3. Steam makes a turbine spin.

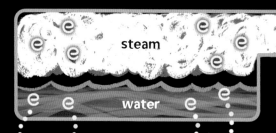

steam

water

turbine

MOTION

FUEL

HEAT

Most power stations use COAL for fuel.

4. The turbine spins a magnet in a generator.

ELECTRICITY

generator

magnet

wire coils

6. The electricity moves through wires to buildings.

When someone needs power, they plug into me!

5. The spinning magnet makes electricity in wire coils.

Notice how the ENERGY changes from
FUEL to HEAT to MOTION to ELECTRICITY.

There's another **BURNING ISSUE** about fossil fuels....

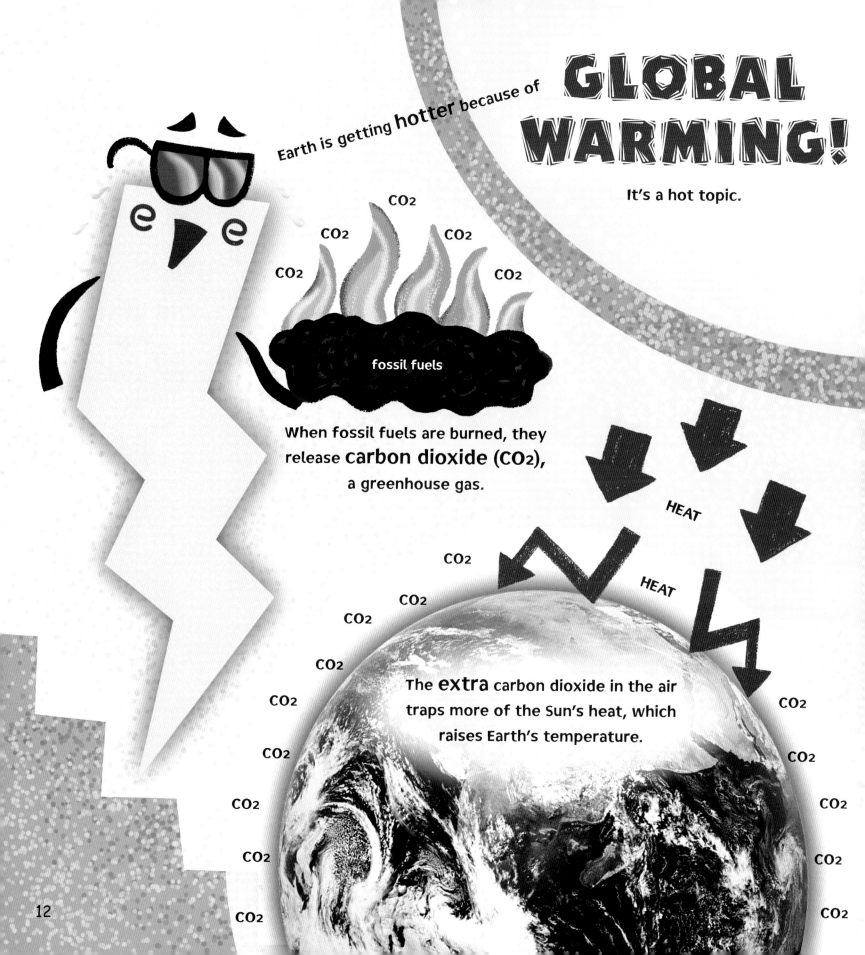

Earth is getting **hotter** because of

GLOBAL WARMING!

It's a hot topic.

CO2 CO2 CO2 CO2 CO2

fossil fuels

When fossil fuels are burned, they release **carbon dioxide (CO2)**, a greenhouse gas.

HEAT

HEAT

CO2 CO2 CO2 CO2

The **extra** carbon dioxide in the air traps more of the Sun's heat, which raises Earth's temperature.

CO2 CO2 CO2 CO2 CO2 CO2 CO2 CO2 CO2 CO2

A warmer Earth means:

higher sea levels

flooded islands and coastlines

disappearing glaciers

melting ice at the poles

stronger storms and more heat waves

crop failures

low water flow in rivers

habitat loss

more deserts

a longer dry season with more wildfires

Many people want to stop warming up Earth, so they want to reduce the use of fossil fuels.

NUCLEAR POWER

uses the ENERGY of atoms.

Atoms contain the tiny particles we are made of.

Erg, am I really made of atoms?

We all are!

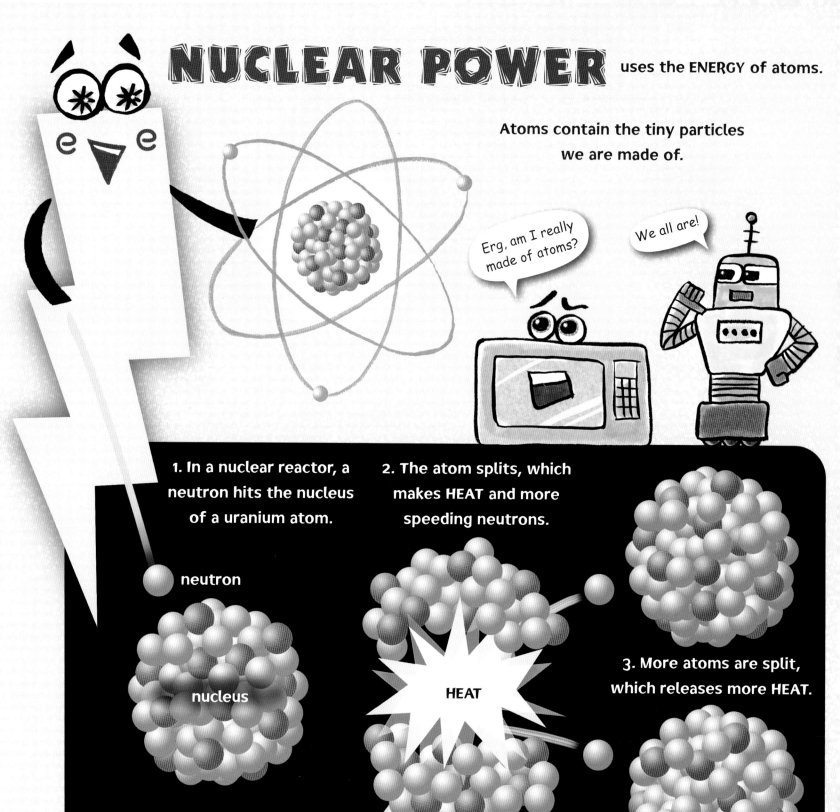

1. In a nuclear reactor, a neutron hits the nucleus of a uranium atom.

neutron

nucleus

Uranium is a toxic, silver-colored metal that is mined from rocks.

2. The atom splits, which makes HEAT and more speeding neutrons.

HEAT

3. More atoms are split, which releases more HEAT.

In a nuclear power plant, the reactor heats water to make steam.

The steam turns a turbine, then a generator makes electricity as in other types of power plants.

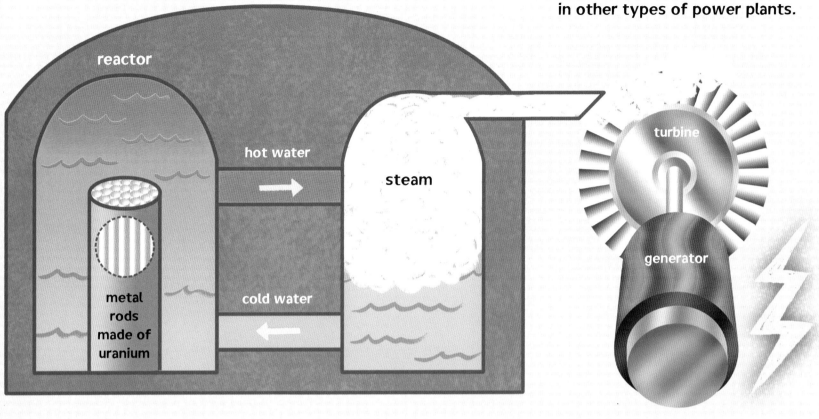

reactor

hot water

steam

metal rods made of uranium

cold water

turbine

generator

Nuclear waste is very **radioactive**. That means it can make people and animals sick (or worse).

Nuclear waste gives everyone a splitting headache!

DANGER RADIOACTIVE WASTE

GOOD NEWS

Nuclear power doesn't cause air pollution or release carbon.

BAD NEWS

The waste from nuclear plants is very dangerous.

Uranium is not renewable, so it will run out.

15

SOLAR POWER

is a **bright** idea!

LIGHT

HEAT

HEAT & LIGHT

The Sun will be shining for **billions** of years. There are many ways to use its ENERGY.

PV panel

PV=photovoltaic

PV panels turn LIGHT into ELECTRICITY.

thermal collector

glass tube style

Thermal collectors absorb HEAT from the Sun.

A passive solar home uses less energy.

It's easy to make hot water using solar energy.

Passive solar buildings are designed to capture LIGHT and HEAT from the Sun as needed.

16

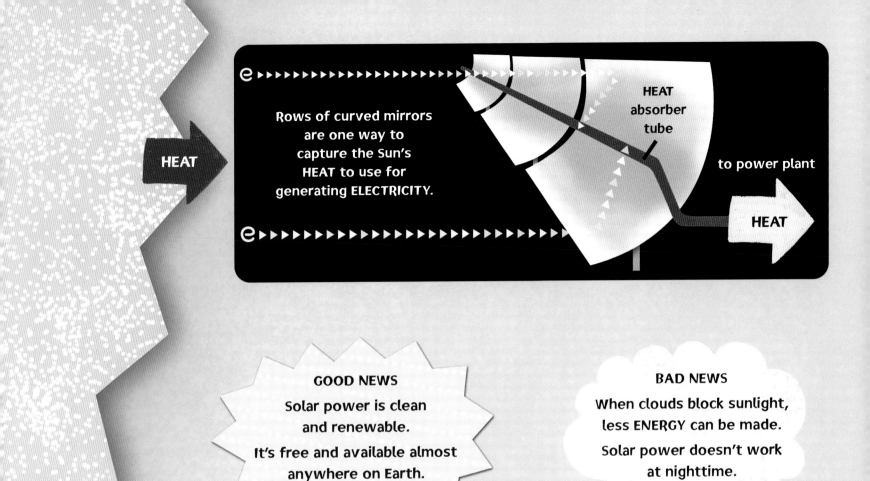

Rows of curved mirrors are one way to capture the Sun's HEAT to use for generating ELECTRICITY.

HEAT absorber tube

to power plant

HEAT

HEAT

GOOD NEWS

Solar power is clean and renewable.

It's free and available almost anywhere on Earth.

BAD NEWS

When clouds block sunlight, less ENERGY can be made.

Solar power doesn't work at nighttime.

What in the world are you?

A solar oven! I don't need electricity, gas, or wood to cook food.

The Sun charges my battery all day so I can shine light at night.

Cool! And I can calculate how much electricity you save.

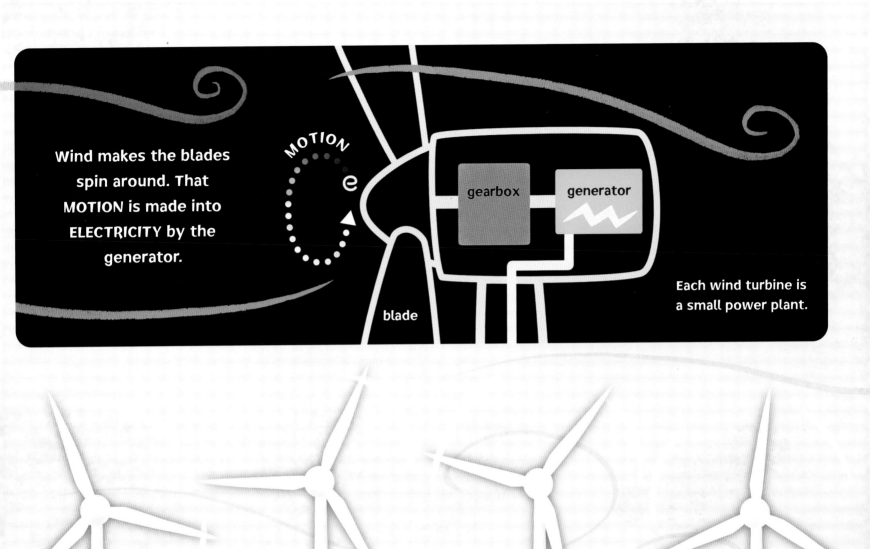

Wind makes the blades spin around. That MOTION is made into ELECTRICITY by the generator.

MOTION

blade

gearbox

generator

Each wind turbine is a small power plant.

A group of turbines is called a **wind farm**.

GOOD NEWS

Wind power is clean and renewable.

It's free and available all over Earth.

BAD NEWS

When the wind isn't blowing, no power can be made.

Some people think wind turbines ruin the view.

WATER POWER is making a splash!

The MOTION of rivers and oceans can provide plenty of ENERGY.

There are many types of hydropower.

"Hydro" means water.

A dam controls a river so the flow of water will turn a turbine to generate ELECTRICITY.

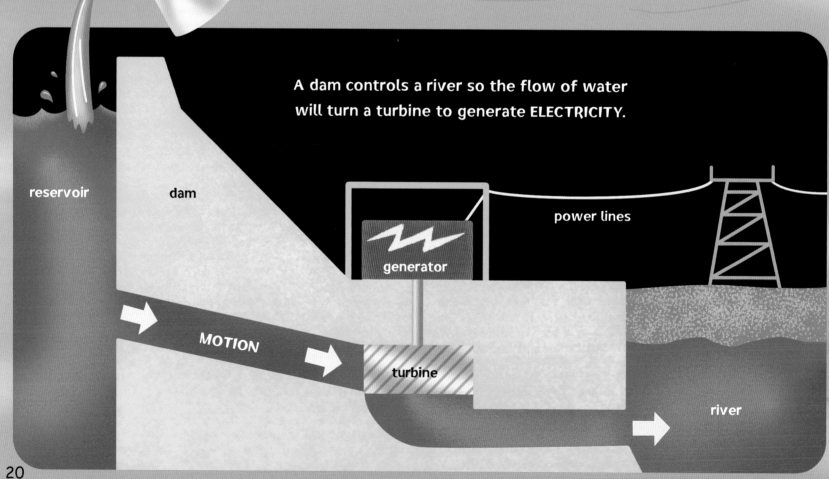

reservoir

dam

generator

power lines

MOTION

turbine

river

3. Air turns a turbine.

4. A generator makes electricity.

MOTION

2. The water pushes air.

turbine

generator

A wave power station turns the MOTION of the ocean into electrical power.

1. The tide surges into a wave power station.

MOTION

GOOD NEWS

Water power is clean and renewable.

The ocean covers more than 70 percent of Earth.

There are many ways to capture the force of moving water.

BAD NEWS

Dams can damage the environment and harm fish and other animals.

If water levels get low, less power can be made.

Underwater turbines are very similar to wind turbines but use water currents to generate power.

Water power is the wave of the future!

GEOTHERMAL POWER

is down to earth!

"Geo" means **earth** and "thermal" means **heat.**

A geothermal power plant uses HEAT from far **underground.**

1. A well is drilled down to an area with very hot rock and steam.

2. The hot steam is piped up to the surface.

3. In the power plant, the steam turns a turbine, then a generator makes electricity.

4. Cool water is returned to the steam reservoir.

steam reservoir 300 to 700°F

HEAT

No matter how hot or cold the outside air is...

...the temperature a few feet underground stays the same all year, about 60°F.

60°F

A **ground heat pump** uses the underground temperature to help cool the house in summer and heat it in winter.

I can make steam!

Ouch!

GOOD NEWS

Geothermal power is clean and works day and night in any weather.

Ground heat pumps can be used in most places.

BAD NEWS

The high underground temperatures needed for geothermal power plants are not available in many areas.

There are many ways to use the power of plants:

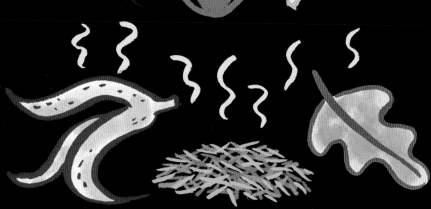

Ethanol is a fuel for running cars and other vehicles that use gasoline.

Ethanol is made from **food crops** such as beets, sugarcane, or corn. Switchgrass, corn stalks, and other **nonedible** plant parts may also be used.

Biogas can be used for heat or to generate electricity instead of natural gas.

Biogas is made from decaying leaves, manure, food scraps, grass clippings, and similar **waste**.

Biodiesel is used in trucks and other vehicles with a diesel engine.

Biodiesel is made from **vegetable oils** and by certain kinds of **algae**.

GOOD NEWS

Plant power is clean and renewable.

Plants can grow in many different places.

Let's make "grassoline"!

BAD NEWS

Plants grown for fuel take up farmland that could grow food, which leads to higher food prices.

ENERGY costs money, and nobody wants to throw money away! So, here are some energy-saving tips for kids and grown-ups:

A light-colored roof keeps the house cooler in summer.

Don't let the refrigerator door hang open.

Buy energy-saving appliances.

Put lids on pots to heat food faster.

Microwaves use less power than ranges.

Give the stove some time off and skip cooking for some meals.

Use natural light during the day.

Seal leaks around windows and doors.

Compact fluorescent bulbs make more light with less power.

Use washable towels.

Fix leaks and don't let water run.

Eat less meat and buy locally grown foods.

Don't buy water in disposable bottles.

Turn OFF lights when you leave the room.

Grass lawns use up money and energy because they need regular watering, fertilizer, and pesticides, plus...

A solar water heater makes hot water without electricity.

An attic fan cools the house in summer.

A smaller house takes less ENERGY to build and operate.

Plant trees to help shade the house in summer and block cold winds in winter.

Trees absorb carbon dioxide, a greenhouse gas that causes global warming.

Insulation keeps the heating and air-conditioning from leaking out.

Turn OFF the computer, TV, and video games and go outside!

Turn OFF fans when no one is in the room.

Unplug cell phone chargers when not in use.

If a room is chilly, wrap up in a blanket or put on a sweater.

Use a power strip to make sure gadgets are really turned OFF.

Hang clothes up to dry instead of using a dryer.

60°

Don't overheat the house in winter.

Use rechargeable batteries.

Wash laundry in cold or warm water, not hot.

Turn down the hot water heater to about 120°F.

Ways to Save Gas:

Walk, run, bike, or ride mass transit instead of driving a car.

Drive a small car.

Drive a hybrid or electric car.

Combine errands into one trip.

Avoid jackrabbit starts.

Keep tires inflated to the proper pressure.

Go the speed limit.

Carpool.

Buy used items when possible. It takes ENERGY to make new stuff.

Bring reusable bags when shopping...

...instead of placing items in throwaway plastic bags.

Recycle!

Donate old toys and clothes to a thrift shop.

So, let's get started, because the truth is, when you **save** ENERGY you also save the **Earth**!

YAY!!!

YAY!!!

YAY!!!

More about ENERGY

Several **forms of energy** are shown on pages 4–5. Another form is potential GRAVITATIONAL energy. An example is snow lying quietly on a hill that could become an avalanche.

Another example is HYDROGEN, which can be used in fuel cells, a type of battery. On Earth, hydrogen doesn't exist naturally in pure form; it's part of something such as water (H_2O). It takes a lot of energy to produce pure hydrogen, but it could be a useful way to store energy and move it around.

The grid moves electricity from power plants to buildings. The thousands of miles of towers, poles, and wires that carry electricity make up the grid. About 10,000 power plants in the U.S. produce the electricity that keeps the lights, TVs, computers, video games, and everything else ON.

The big problem is, **there's no way to store electricity on a large scale.** Electricity has to be produced as needed and then sent out over the grid right away. Unfortunately, much of the grid is old, wastes electricity, and needs to be replaced, which is a huge expense. Many people want to build a "smart grid" designed to waste less energy, use renewable power sources, and reduce outages.

Web links:
Energy Information Administration Kid's Page
www.eia.doe.gov/kids/
This site has information about energy sources, activities, and units. For example, did you know that 1 barrel of oil = 42 gallons?

EERE Kids Saving Energy
www.eere.energy.gov/kids/
Games, tips, and facts about renewables. Energy Efficiency and Renewable Energy is part of the U.S. Dept. of Energy. This page has projects such as making a solar oven from a pizza box: www1.eere.energy.gov/education/science_projects.html

NEED Science Fair Projects
www.need.org/energyfair.php
The National Energy Education and Development website has many additional resources for teachers and students, including downloadable curricula and activity guides.

A note about Erg's name:
an **erg** is a unit for measuring energy.

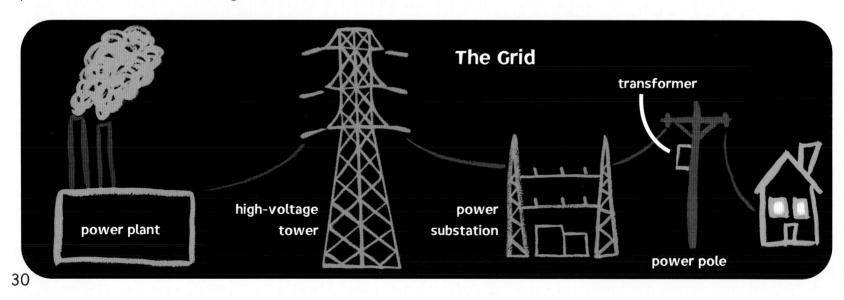

The Grid

power plant

high-voltage tower

power substation

transformer

power pole

More about saving ENERGY (and money!)

How does saving water save energy?
Water must be cleaned, stored, and pumped a long way to come out of your faucet. The energy to heat water for showers, washing machines, and dishwashers is a big part of the average power bill. One tip: short showers take less water than baths.

What's wrong with bottled water?
It takes a great deal of energy to put water inside bottles, transport it to stores, then to your home. Plain bottled water often costs more per gallon than gasoline. The plastic bottle is only used once, then discarded. It's much better to use a travel mug or thermos that can be filled over and over again with tap water.

Recycling is a green thing to do, right?
Yes, but it takes energy to recycle bottles, newspapers, and other recyclables. It's much better to avoid the need for it if possible. For example, online newspapers, catalogs, or phone directories as well as reusable containers don't require recycling.

What's better about eating local?
The average food item on dinner plates in the U.S. has been shipped hundreds of miles from where it was grown. Eating locally grown foods saves quite a bit of energy. In addition, organic foods use much less fossil fuel than conventionally farmed food.

Why is it good to buy used things?
It takes quite a bit of energy to make new products. The raw materials must be gathered, made into something, then shipped somewhere. Buying used things takes much less energy.

Is it really turned OFF?
Many TVs, video games, and other gadgets use some power even when they're turned off. If the item has a remote control, it uses electricity all the time. If it has a clock or tiny lights glowing, it's always ON.

The block-shaped adapters and chargers also use power when they're plugged into an outlet. For example, a cell phone charger uses power even if the phone itself is not attached.

One way to turn any gadget completely OFF is to unplug it from the outlet. Another idea is to plug it into a power strip that has an ON/OFF switch.

Does it matter if one kid tries to save energy?
Yes! Turning off a light once only saves a few cents' worth of energy, but turning off unneeded lights for the rest of your life saves much more. It's true for all the changes we make to reduce our energy use—they add up to big savings!

Sources for this book include the U.S. Department of Energy and the Energy Information Administration.

More Bad News about Fossil Fuels

All energy sources have their pros and cons, some of which are mentioned in this book. Oil, natural gas, and coal currently provide most of the world's energy. Because **fossil fuels are not renewable**, sooner or later people will have to switch to other forms of power. If we don't plan ahead and begin the changeover, **shortages will cause big problems**.

Oil (petroleum) is the #1 source of fuels for cars, trucks, trains, boats, and airplanes. Drilling for oil has been going on for more than 150 years, so the **easiest-to-drill deposits were located long ago**. Most older oil fields are empty or running low. For example, oil production in the United States has declined every year since 1972. At this writing, around 70 percent of the oil consumed by Americans is imported from other countries.

The terms "oil sands" and "shale oil" describe substances that are NOT the same as conventional petroleum (which is a fluid.) In areas where sand or mudstone do contain oil, it's all mixed together. **A huge amount of water and energy** is needed to separate out the oil. The result is a heavy crude oil that does not flow easily, which makes it difficult to transport or turn into fuels. The large-scale mining of these heavy oil-precursors would result in vast quantities of rock waste, greater pollution, and more carbon dioxide release as compared to conventionally drilled oil.

The Good News Is: People Can Switch to Green Power!

Compressed natural gas (CNG) can be used to power vehicles. While less polluting than gasoline and diesel, **like all fossil fuels it releases carbon**, a greenhouse gas that causes global warming. In the United States, natural gas is primarily used in power plants to generate electricity.

Coal mining is often **dangerous for workers** and very **environmentally destructive**. One of the worst practices is mountaintop removal, which turns mountains into piles of rubble. The term "clean coal" is used to describe various ways people are trying to make coal less polluting. While some methods can work (such as reducing sulfur), most of the other technologies are unproven, expensive, take extra energy, and leave toxic waste behind.

For these and other reasons, many people want to use less fossil fuel and use more renewable power such as solar, wind, and geothermal. But the **biggest power resource** in the U.S. today is increased efficiency. In other words...

Use LESS energy!

Turn us OFF!